FOLLOWING THE LEADER

A Guide for Planning
Founding Director Transition

❧

Emily Redington
Donn F. Vickers

❧

Acknowledgements

Most of all we hope this report works for you. If it does it is largely because of the generous reflections and considerable insights of board members, staff, and executives in five agencies. Their transition stories and learnings have formed the substance of what follows.

Our particular thanks to Paula DiPerna of The Joyce Foundation for believing it was worth doing and to our lively project committee who saw that it was done well. We thank the board and staff of the Academy for Leadership and Governance and The Jefferson Center for creating an atmosphere that is hospitable to creative and thoughtful work.

Finally, this looks smart because of our designer Cyndi Daines and reads smoothly because of our editor Elizabeth Jewell.

Emily Redington
Donn Vickers
Summer, 2001

Table of Contents

Chapter I

An Introduction

Greg Stein could have been a teacher. Instead he poured his considerable imagination and large-sized commitment to central city youth into starting TeenWorks. It was 1974. His own idealism born in the previous decade was still intact and he believed that tutoring, advising, and relating personally to out-of-school youth could change, even save young lives. Now, twenty-seven years later, TeenWorks serves more than two thousand kids a year, has a staff of fourteen full- and part-time counselors and instructors, and a budget of just under $1-million.

Now Greg is ready to move on. At age fifty-eight he's not ready for retirement, but is more than ready for a different way of working and living. He does worry about what will happen to TeenWorks. The organization has been shaped by his personality, his way of managing, even his kind of people hired as colleagues. He wants the organization to continue to prosper, but what can he do? How can he make sure that his successor and the board will move on beyond the long shadow of his tenure?

This report is for Greg and others like him.

Amelia Brown has been on the board of TeenWorks for seven years. As director of human resources at a local bank she knows about young employees, about work and learning. She also knows that TeenWorks has been a very good thing for a lot of people. She has returned to the board for another six-year term because she greatly admires Greg and believes in what the organization has been able to accomplish under his leadership.

But she sometimes wonders whether the organization is too much dependant on Greg's leadership, too much an extension of his personality. Since Greg has announced he is leaving, her wondering has turned to worry. Is there anyone else out there like him that can keep the place going? Should the board even look for someone unlike him? What kind of person can be successful after a passionate founding leader like Greg? How will the board orient this person and prepare her for all the challenges ahead?

This report is for Amelia and others like her.

Marcia Sanchez has been a middle school principal for twelve years. She had volunteered at TeenWorks while teaching in the joint vocational school. She liked what they did and how they did it. She didn't really know Greg but was well aware of how many did know and respect him. She had often thought it would be nice to work in a place like that, focusing on truly needy kids and having the freedom to do whatever seemed best. So when she heard Greg was leaving she thought about applying. She knew he was popular, she knew the whole organization had been formed according to his vision, and she knew the popular wisdom that it is only the successor to the successor that succeeds.

How would she know to take the job if offered? Would she consult with Greg? Should she keep staff clearly loyal to him? Could she imagine putting her own stamp on the organization? How long would that take?

This report is for Marcia and others like her.

The departure of a founding director is no small matter. Founders, board members, and potential successors have legitimate questions and concerns that deserve attention. What is it that we know about this phenomenon of founding executive succession? What can we say to those who experience it? In what follows we write for those founding directors, board members, and successors who are having this powerful transition experience.

We also write out of the experience of others like you who know the power of long-term directorates and the issues related to bringing them to a successful conclusion: Those individuals have also wondered what to do and worried about how a new executive will fit. This report is for all of you, since long-term directorate transitions have many or all of the characteristics and therefore challenges of those associated with the founding director. So while this document refers to the "founding director," it is fair to read "long-term director" when that phrase is used.

What you will find here is based on the literature about executive succession. It is also based on a series of on-site interviews organized around an interview schedule and carefully recorded. These interviews were done with selected organizations that had been through the succession of a founding director, and we made sure we talked with the founders, key board members, and the successors who had experienced that transition. The details of that interview process and the literature review are contained in the appendices.

However, this is not "fully standardized" research with impeccable methodology written for academicians or for publication in a journal, though such work can be of great value to practitioners. But in what follows, we honor another kind of value: a first-hand report to the field based on the experiences and best practices of others in the field.

That is what this report contains: founding directors, board members, and successors reflecting on this significant organizational transition and trying to discern what works, what doesn't, and how it might be done better. You will read the advice and counsel of people like you, in organizations like yours, who have been somewhere like where you are, done something like you are doing, and have learned some lessons worth sharing in the process.

You'll notice we say *we*. In this document there are three levels of we: the two of us writing, an additional five that form the project committee, and the larger circle of executives, board members, and successors whose voices we have recorded from interviews.

Donn Vickers is the founding director of two organizations and presently concluding his twenty-year tenure at one. Emily Redington is now Assistant Director of a cultural institution having recently completed a Master's thesis on founding director succession.

The project committee includes two board members with direct experience in executive transition, two executives, (both founders, one in the late and one in the early stages of transition,) and a graduate student who knows a thing or two about research.

The people in the field who were part of the survey are at the center of it all. Their thoughtfulness about their own transition experiences and their willingness to share their learnings make them the most royal and appreciated we of this project.

If you read the table of contents you will discover that, depending on your role in the organization, Chapter III, IV, or V will be more helpful to you. If you are in the early stages of your transition, the first part of Chapter II on Succession Planning will not be too late. Wherever you are, the Succession Process outlined at the end of Chapter II will probably be of use. Do look at the literature review in Appendix A. There are strong parallels elsewhere that you may wish to explore. Finally, we end with a word about leadership. That is after all what it will take from all parties to make the transition a successful and satisfying one. We wish you well as you try to discover and discern what leadership in your situation will mean for you and the organization of which you are a part.

Chapter II
Succession Planning

Making the transition from a founding director to new executive leadership is no small undertaking. Few people would argue against the need to plan when facing such a crucial moment in an organization's life. Still, before you begin to plan, it will help to make clear who should be involved and when you want to start. This chapter begins with that discussion, offering several ideas for the composition of your planning committee and then sharing recommendations for succession planning from our interviewees. The final section of the chapter outlines one potential succession process, and then offers an example of a succession timeline used by one of the organizations we studied.

We recommend that when you begin thinking about succession planning, you also consider strategic planning. The future of your organization's executive leadership is closely tied to the future of your organization as a whole, and the most successful succession plans we've seen are part of a larger strategic plan. Even if you've never done such a plan before, a time of organizational change offers the opportunity you need to make strategic planning a priority.

Who should do this planning?

Most would agree that the leaders in your organization ought to initiate and continue the planning. That includes the board president, usually the board officers and/or the full executive committee, and possibly two or more past presidents. Some organizations we interviewed chose to involve the founding director in the planning process, while others preferred that the founder serve only in an advisory role. Beyond these key leaders, it is your call based on your history of planning and the amount of time your organization can apply to it.

The succession plans we saw were carefully selective, involving the executive committee, other key board members, and staff. Some included a few individuals external to the organization such as volunteers, audience members, clients, funders, or representatives from government agencies or appointing authorities. Not all of these people need to participate at the same level and in the same way. They may respond in interviews, focus groups, or questionnaires, or they may react to draft documents.

As with any committee within your organization, you will want to include individuals from diverse age, gender, and racial backgrounds. But diversity in your planning process also includes diversity in organizational functions, meaning involving those who perform anything from marketing to programming to fundraising roles. When making these selections it is important to keep in mind that you may be asked to explain to the rest of the organization why you are selecting certain people and by implication not selecting others. The key is having the right mix and that means including some who may resist change or may be critical of the founder.

Recommendations from the field

Like any planning process, there are elements of succession planning that are of major importance and others that are of comparatively moderate or low importance. At the end of each of our interviews, we asked our interviewees to give recommendations as to what they felt were the most important factors leading to successful transition. Here are the most frequently mentioned responses:

1. Time.

Almost all interviewees mentioned adequate planning time as essential to the success of their transitions. Lead time helps members of your organization not only to plan for leadership change but also to grow accustomed to the reality of the founder's retirement. How much time you need depends on your organization's unique needs; responses to this question varied among interviewees. One founder indicated that a full three years' notice was appropriate, while another thought that two years was a bit longer than necessary. Most agreed that a margin of at least eighteen months prior to the founder's retirement is preferred to handle the complexity of succession planning, while overextending the process beyond a few years can create 'lame duck' leadership issues.

2. Be clear about the qualities sought in the new executive.

This is especially true with founding director succession because of the tendency to compare candidates to the founder. Interviewees found frank discussion between board members and possibly a consultant about the executive director position essential to creating an accurate description of the qualities needed and sought. Regardless of whether the founder contributes personally to such a discussion, it should include as much openness about the position and the organization's needs as possible.

3. Involve all segments of the organization's community.

As mentioned earlier, relying on the strength, knowledge, and expertise of your staff, board members, volunteers, and clients in times of change contributes to the success of your transition. If these people feel involved in the transition process, they are more likely to embrace the successor's leadership.

4. Communicate.

Fear of the unknown is a common human and organizational reaction. When members of an organization are not provided information about the progress of the transition, they feel closed off from the process and without control in their own environment. Even if they have no decision-making role in the transition, being aware of the process can help them approach the change with comfort and confidence.

5. Stay close to the mission of the organization.

This can help keep the planning process on track and ensure that despite the changes underway in the organization, all of its members are unified under a common goal. As one successor commented, "Everything we do comes out of our mission," whether programming or grant-writing or strategic planning. The mission statement is a key way to view your organization as a separate entity from the founder, smoothing the way for the transition.

6. Have a vision for the planning process.

Often organizations place such emphasis on visionary programming that they overlook visionary planning. Having a goal in mind for the process itself, independent of your organization's larger operations, helps you identify what the organization needs not only to get through the transition but to do so confidently and find the right person for the job.

A potential succession process

Throughout this report we stress the need for you to develop a transition that works best for your organization. We have gathered insights and suggestions from others who have experienced founding director transition firsthand and we think they can be helpful. You may want to use a little, some, or all of what you see below.

Pre-succession steps:

1. The founder makes the decision to retire. In the best-case scenario there would be at least eighteen months notice prior to retirement to allow for a thorough planning and search process. In each case we looked at, founders presented their decision to retire to the board and the staff before making the decision known to the community.

2. The board appoints a planning committee. The committee would ideally be working both on a succession plan and the organization's overarching strategic plan, which would make the transition part of a larger vision for the organization. The planning committee likely would consist of board members, both past and present, and key volunteers (see "Who should do this planning?" on page 5 for a more thorough discussion of the composition of the planning committee). It could also include an external consultant with experience in leadership searches. This group's task is to develop a general timeline of the progression of the executive search. In conjunction with the staff and in some cases the founder, the committee either creates or updates the executive director's job description, and then identifies the abilities and characteristics desired in the new leader. Any projects associated with the transition, such as the formalization of an organizational history or the identification of an explicit organizational culture, would be named and developed around this time. The work of the planning committee would ideally be concluded at least one year prior to the founder's retirement.

3. The board appoints a search committee. This committee usually includes some members of the planning committee, as well as some board members with experience in executive searches or human resources. Members of the search committee can review the timeline, job description, and executive abilities and characteristics outlined by the planning committee and use that work to guide their next steps. Ideally this committee would be in place at least six months before the founder retires.

4. The search committee advertises the position, collects resumes, and conducts interviews. Typically the search committee is responsible for the publicity surrounding the position, including advertising, special events and announcements, or the use of any external executive search tools, such as headhunters. After collecting resumes, the committee will want to create a process through which all candidates can be fairly reviewed and develop an interview procedure for top candidates. This portion of the transition ideally would be completed four or five months before the founder's retirement.

5. The search committee reviews finalists, some of whom are then called for second interviews. At this point the search committee may wish to introduce the finalists to other members of the organization, including staff, so that they better understand the position, the people, and the environment. Ordinarily the review of finalists would take place with three to four months remaining.

6. The new executive director is hired. This person may or may not expect an employment contract. The candidate should be selected, contract negotiated, and start date determined at least one month before the founder's retirement.

Transition steps:

1. The founder can choose to spend up to one month with the new leader in the executive director position. This gives both individuals the opportunity to set a positive tone for the transition, and reduces the likelihood of unforeseen problems hampering the new leader's effectiveness following the founder's departure. Several of the organizations we interviewed used this overlap period to promote the success of the new executive. Others chose not to use this approach, indicating that they felt a clean break was necessary to ensure that the new leader would be in charge from the first day.

2. The successor is formally and informally introduced to organizational members, community leaders, donors, and colleagues. This raises the new leader's public presence, and if the founder chooses to make the introductions the successor gains the founder's "stamp of approval" when taking charge. Several of the founders and successors we interviewed indicated that this was an important tool both for founders and for the new leaders, each of whom felt more comfortable about the transition following the introduction and training period. Others felt that introductions could be performed by board and staff members instead.

3. The founder remains in contact with the successor on a consultant basis for a brief period (perhaps up to six months) following retirement. As mentioned in (1), having the founder available to the new executive for advice or information reduces the chances of unforeseen problems becoming crises for the organization. It also makes all members of the organization feel more comfortable about the ability of the successor to problem-solve in early months when information and experience may be scarce. However, the consultant role must be approached carefully. If the founder maintains too much contact with the organization, that may undermine or interfere with the work of the new leader and make the founder's process of letting go more difficult. None of the interviewees indicated that this aspect of continued involvement proved problematic at any stage of the transition process, probably due to the very conscientious way each founder approached the consultant role.

Post-succession steps:

1. The successor should allow an extended period of time (as much as two years) to learn the position, the organizational culture, and the community. Many aspects of organizational life take months to unfold, and several new executives we interviewed highlighted the importance of accepting and even expecting some uncertainty well into any successor's tenure.

2. The successor should also allow for a "grieving" period following the founder's departure. This holds true both internally and externally, and depends on the way the founder was viewed. A timeframe of approximately six months is a good benchmark for this period, during which the successor would attempt to keep major change to a minimum and focus on learning the job, the intricacies of the organization, and the external environment.

3. The successor can make smaller changes within the organization when they are necessary in order to perform the executive's job effectively. The new leader is formalizing a position within the organization that had been designed around the skills of a particular leader, and the successor's persona, style, and approach may not resemble the founder's. In one organization we interviewed, the founder was described as a manager who was very involved in the activities of her subordinates; her successor considers himself an "anti-manager" and takes a hands-off approach to management. The successor should not feel pressure to conform to systems bequeathed by the founder when those systems do not match the successor's personal management style. In fact, it is to the benefit of the organization that the new executive does not attempt such a conformation.

4. The successor should try to understand existing work styles and procedures in the organization and formalize those procedures that seem to work well. These procedures are not always codified under the founder, and the successor can take meaningful action in the first months of tenure by formalizing those aspects of organizational life that are positive and effective for staff, board, and volunteers. In this way, the successor can establish a leadership style and avoid the appearance that the organization is simply in a holding pattern following the transition.

5. If possible, all members of the organization should avoid comparisons between the founder and the successor. Taking a position previously held by a founding director is akin to swimming in uncharted depths. As is the case with any person in any job, there are bound to be widely disparate opinions and evaluations of the founder's leadership style, strengths and weaknesses, choice of emphasis, and so on. These opinions should not be transferred to the new executive or used as a benchmark for success or failure.

An example of a succession and search timeline

Here's how one organization we know designed the timeline for replacing the founding director.

1. Name and convene search committee: June 2000

2. Create position description and design recruitment/selection strategy: June – July 2000

3. Develop promotional and application materials: August 2000

4. Disseminate promotional and application materials: September 1, 2000

5. Application deadline: October 31, 2000 or until filled

6. Review applications, invite candidates for interviews and issue "thank you, but no" letters: November – December 2000

7. Conduct interviews: January 2001

8. Evaluate interviews and check references: end of January – February 15, 2001

9. Make contract offer: February 15, 2001

10. Contract signed: March 1, 2001

11. New executive director starts: June 1, 2001

Developing a succession process and timeline is hard work that will demand time, thought, and energy. One organization we interviewed took almost six months to develop a plan before it was presented to the board, and then another three months (and two board meetings) before the plan was approved. Your succession plan won't be written in one meeting, but if done right, it will serve your organization well into the tenure of the next executive.

Chapter III
For the Board

To hold in trust the mission of an organization may be the highest purpose of a Board of Trustees. It is particularly crucial at the time of the founding director's departure. Founding executives often seem and act as if they own the mission. They were there in the beginning, they formulated the vision, and over the years they have embodied that mission and represented the organization in the community. In fact, organizations need leaders with energy and imagination if they are to be successful. But leaders who do not engage, inspire, and incorporate others in the mission and life of the organization are preparing the way for an executive transition full of difficulties. Founding directors who try to single-handedly hold in trust the mission of the organization create boards which are not practiced at owning and caring for the mission and are, therefore, ill-equipped to take hold at a time of executive succession.

Whatever amount of leadership you as a board have shared with your executive in the past, now, at this critical time of founding director transition, is when you must choose to lead. It may require a retreat or outside consultation; it certainly will require extra time and renewed commitment to the life and mission of your organization. You will not want to exclude your executive but you will want to make it clear that leadership for the transition process is yours. You are the ones who will remain and be entrusted with the organization's life and mission. You are the ones therefore who must take charge, lead, and assume full responsibility for the well-being of the organization.

It has been our experience — through conversation with boards going through the departure of their founding director — that there are some things which seem to make a difference. What we found was that organizations that had relatively successful transitions had boards that took strong and thoughtful leadership in five areas. Depending on your organization's situation, different ones of them will be more or less important. All five areas are worthy of your review.

1. Planning.

You may have four to eighteen months as a transition period. What you do from the time you know your executive is leaving until the departure is of course important. Better yet is that the plan for the transition period is embedded in a two- to three-year plan for the organization. Here's one scenario that seemed to work well: Upon hearing that the founding executive would leave in eighteen months the board appointed a strategic planning committee comprised of present and past board members. Their charge was to develop a comprehensive plan for all aspects of the organization that included the time period of the transition and two years beyond. This approach placed the activity of the transition in the broader context of an ongoing plan for the life of the organization. It was helpful in that it did not isolate the transition period from the important work to follow and it was useful in providing fresh information about the direction of the organization for prospective candidates for the executive position.

This plan involved special attention to capturing the existing culture of the organization. Lively board and staff conversations about "who we are and what we wish to preserve" enabled the board to broaden and deepen its understanding and therefore to be better able to exert the necessary leadership. These conversations were useful to the founding director ("They do know what we are all about") and useful as well to prospective candidates who inquired about the special personality and culture of the organization.

2. Transition Purposes.

There are some obvious and unavoidable things that need to be done during the transition that relate to honoring the departing executive and searching for the new one. It is important for the transition period to have a purpose that goes beyond these necessary tasks of search and celebration. Some suggestions follow. One organization consolidated two of its programs into one to save time and resources. Another sought and received funds to initiate a new program for teenage youth, an audience not previously served. Another added additional staff meetings to do training that broadened the scope of what each staff member knew and could do. Still another spent six months re-working and renewing one of its basic programs.

The point of all this is to keep the organization alive and developing during the transition. The work of transition is important work but must not be allowed to be the only, certainly not the primary, work that the organization does. Those interviewed shared the belief that the transition as a whole works better when it does not consume all the creative energies of the organization. Organizational programs, processes, staffing, and systems cannot be permitted to be dormant during an extended succession transition. The work of the organization must continue.

3. The Search.

What follows are a few basics that seemed to many to be important aspects of an effective search process.

Think about representation. For most organizations, a search committee of five to nine members is about right. That means careful thinking about who those few are. Apart from obvious age, gender, and race considerations, you should consider selecting people who represent different aspects of the organization (programming, marketing, elected officers, for example), new and seasoned board members, those with different points of view, formal and informal leaders, and those with previous search experience as well as some who are fresh to the task.

Be clear about the charge. What are the guidelines and givens that the board has established? Now is the time to know (or ask) and be particularly clear about:

- a preliminary job description
- the salary range
- the benefit package
- the committee's budget and expenses
- the geographical scope of the search
- acceptability of "inside" candidates
- preferred date for the new executive to begin
- particular skills or traits deemed as important from the organization's assessment
- the use of a search consultant
- whether one or multiple candidates are to be recommended and slated for board review
- process and responsibility for final selection
- the point at which the committee completes its work.

Begin with your own valuable experience. Many of you have chosen executives before. You already have ideas about what you are looking for and how to go about getting it. Think about your interaction with other organizational executives. Who are the best you have known? What about them earned your respect? What conclusions have you drawn about effective leaders from those experiences? Narrow your conclusions from sentences to words or phrases. What are the five or ten words that best describe what you think is important in an executive?

Now, be negative. Most of us have had bad experiences, and are quite sure of things we want to avoid. Again, spare the long story in favor of the phrase. Be clear about traits you dislike. Perhaps you can finish a sentence like "I don't want to select someone who is _____" or "Executives I find most difficult are those who _____."

Create a pool of diverse candidates. You must do this if you are going to draw attractive candidates, including those who may not be actively on the job market. The position needs to be touted, advertised, and spoken about through all the informal networks of colleagues, professional associations, past board members, funders, and community institutions. Have an open discussion in the committee about gender, race, and age. This is not "what does the law require" (although that is worth discussing), but what do the mix of values and organizational requirements suggest? What do you care about? What do you wish to make sure you communicate about yourselves by this process? The search committee must pursue a diversity of sources in order to assure a rich mix of fine candidates.

Develop an application. What do you want to know before deciding to meet this candidate? Many standard applications are available to review, and since the business of writing resumes is thriving, you no doubt will receive plenty. Many candidates show skill in resume writing far beyond skill in leadership. Often, our experience is that because of many factors (such as long application forms and dazzling resumes), searchers end up with non-crucial information not easily comparable from candidate to candidate. You probably can't avoid the resume rush, but you can devise a simple required application to give you information to compare.

Three categories of questions that we have found to be of particular value are: 1.) questions that get at the candidate's degree of self-assessment and reflection, 2.) those that probe the candidate's way of working, and 3.) those that point toward the candidate's sense of your mission. Example questions for each category follow:

- *Self-reflection and assessment*
What are you best at as a leader and what skills are you still developing? What would your present board say about your leadership ability and style?

- *Way of working*
Describe how you work with your board president and board. How often would you have staff meetings and what would be the chief purposes of those sessions?

- *Sense of mission*
How would you describe the mission of our organization? What aspects of our mission and program would you be most likely to adjust or change? Why?

4. Stability.

While there is not one best way to run an organization, a transition period presents a good time to get more clear and ordered around systems, structures, staffing, and financial stability. We found that many organizations run by a strong founding executive relied too much on the sheer will and energy of the executive. Things worked but mostly because of the large presence of the founder. As a result things like systems, structures, and staffing were loose to informal. One organization decided that the transition was a good time to rewrite position descriptions as a way of better clarifying the work of the staff. Another organization reworked the structure and responsibility of board committees and chairs. Another involved an enlarged fund development committee in reviewing and assessing all the sources of funding and deciding on some new strategies that included a greater number of board members.

Just as a time of transition is a time to continue to do the creative work of the organization, it is also a time to clarify, organize, and sharpen the systems and procedures that keep the organization fit. It is important work in and of itself as it lays important groundwork for the new executive leadership.

5. Rituals.

You may want to create rituals. According to many they seem to be an important aspect of marking the departure of a founder and the arrival of a new executive. You as a board need to determine what is a natural fit for your organization — the degree of formality and fun, the extent to which you will merge the personal and the professional.

Consider who it is that needs to say goodbye to the founding director in a celebratory way. Depending on the size of your town or city and how public a figure your executive has been, it could be that you go beyond the board and close constituents to the broader community. When and if that seems like the right way you may then have to create another setting in which the "immediate family" of the organization has the chance to honor the founder in a more personal way. Again, it is for you to decide what best works in your situation — what is the best mix of celebration and tribute, of written and oral communications, of mementos and gifts. It will be a major passage for your organization and it will likely feel more completed and concluded if you pay attention to some rituals in which those important to your organization can participate.

Chapter IV

For the Founding Executive

Now a new kind of leadership is required. It is not the leadership of imagining a new thing, or creating, building, sustaining, and renewing that thing. Your organization and all that you have done over the years no doubt bears your own special stamp as a result. Its culture is the outgrowth of your personality and its ways have been your ways. But now your leader wisdom needs to focus on a new set of issues. The new issues can be categorized by two kinds of challenges: *the leadership of preparing the way* and *the leadership of letting go.*

We assume that you care deeply about your organization, its people, and its mission. We assume as well that you care just as deeply that it continues, flourishes, even grows into new forms. Most importantly, we assume that while you have enjoyed being well-regarded for what you, your board, and your staff have accomplished, you hope for your successor a similar high regard. All that being true, we have extracted from interviews and experience an even eight things for you to consider. They are eight factors that seem to have an ongoing effect on your organization as it will exist beyond your own leadership. The first three of the factors pertain to the time before the succession period, four, five, and six relate to that time when the succession is in progress, and seven and eight apply after you have completed your obligations to the organization.

These eight factors are at least a good starting point. They may suggest some particular action on your part, such as reviewing them with a trusted colleague. Our bottom line belief is that just as the success of your organization has depended upon your own steady involvement, the success of this leadership transition will be deeply influenced by your own attitudes and actions. Your leadership now is the leadership of preparing the way and the leadership of letting go.

And so here are the factors for your thoughtful reflection.

A) Factors before the succession time period

1. Term: The length of time that you have been the executive.

It is not uncommon that founding directors start and then serve an organization for two or three decades. It does make a difference. In general the longer you have shaped and lived in your organizational house, the more it reflects your own leadership and personality. As a result, the staff, board, and close constituents tend to think of you and the organization as one and the same. Since you cannot go back and quit seven years earlier, you are left with trying to understand the amount and breadth of influence you have had and what you can now do about it to prepare the way for the next executive. Some of that which you can do is addressed in what follows.

2. Belovedness: The organization's view of the founder on a continuum of "dearly beloved" to "enough already."

It may be difficult to keep your humility in check enough to adequately assess this one. The impact can be intense and far-reaching. Founders who stay beyond their point of energy and effectiveness rob themselves of graceful and genuinely celebratory departures. They also drag the organization down with their inordinate focus on their own needs and insufficient attention to the needs of the organization. Transitions go better and organizations remain more successful when founders and their boards mutually agree upon a departure time and schedule that serves well both the needs of the organization and the executive.

3. Notice: The length of time before departing that the executive and board understand and agree upon.

The answer to how much time and how much notice you should give must be 'it depends.' There are many factors including the health of the organization and the relative effectiveness of the executive. Generally we have found that twelve to eighteen months is a reasonable period. Much more than that and the transition loses its energy and the executive may be perceived as "still hanging around." Much less than that and there is not enough time to prepare for and carry out a search which is easily a nine- to twelve-month endeavor.

It is important to remember that if you have been there 20–25 years, giving notice is one thing, while taking it in fully is another. It is not uncommon for boards to take three or four months to fully accept the reality and get on to the important business of a transition plan and an executive search. All that suggests a more relaxed and thoughtful period of time.

B) Factors during succession

4. Management Modification: Degree to which the founding director begins to modify management behaviors related to authority and prominence.

In short the issue here is whether you act as full charge boss to the end. Needless to say that is not the leadership of preparing the way. Whatever your leadership and management style has been over the years, after you have given notice of your departure it is time for change. Change in this case means things like more coaching, less supervising, more delegating, less control, more and broader board involvement, less individual authority and responsibility, and generally moving toward detachment and a comfortable confidence in the staff and board leadership. For one founder this meant working some from home and investing more time in outside projects, limiting the number of hours spent in the office to increase the staff and board's independence.

Further, we have found it important that the departing founder not only move in these directions but talk about these new behaviors. The danger is that the new approach unexplained may be interpreted as disinterest or as having moved on emotionally, but in fact quite the opposite is true. It is a new kind of leadership that continues to care about the organization and its people by preparing the way.

5. Transition Projects: Degree to which the founder takes on specific new initiatives related to stabilizing the organization.

This is a major determinator in the leadership of preparing the way for success. With any luck the organization is already in relatively good shape. There will, however, always remain things that you can do to further strengthen what is already in place. Some examples.

Staffing – Make changes in allocation of responsibility, sharpen and clarify job descriptions, spend time doing the coaching that will broaden and deepen individual staff member ability to perform.

Systems and Procedures – No doubt much of this works because you devised it and made it go forward. Also, no doubt much of it is unwritten. Write it down! Solicit board and staff participation in getting it clear and getting it written.

Finance and Funding – This is likely a place where you have been mostly in charge. Part of what that means is that few if any others know what goes on here and exactly how it is done. Now is the time to further involve board members in knowing and sharing these responsibilities. You may even wish to bring a qualified staff person in on some of the detail of budget building management and fundraising.

All the above and more are aimed at strengthening and stabilizing the organization in anticipation of your departure. This is the leadership of preparing the way for success.

6. Transition Messages: Degree to which the founding director communicates:
- that change is good for the organization and for me
- a positive plan for the next stage of their life
- confidence in the transition process and the new director.

The leadership of preparing the way is the place to start. There is an additional leadership requirement of the executive: the leadership of letting go. The above messages are powerful ones and likely to have a major impact on the success of the transition. In the situations that work best the founder has arrived with the board at the conclusion that moving on is a good thing for the founder and the organization and that now is a good time. If you as a founder feel pushed out on somebody else's timetable that will be a challenge to accept and be positive. But if you depart after 20 plus years in the mode of a victim, that will have significant bearing on the unity and health of the organization.

Secondly, going to something about which you can be glad is far to be desired over going to nothing about which you are anxious. This is a matter of personal preservation and self-respect, but as much a matter of the organization feeling right and comfortable about your departure. Whatever kind of planner you have been in the past, as you approach this transition you owe it to yourself and the organization to have a positive plan for your future.

The final message of import is conveying confidence in those carrying out the transition process and confidence that the new director will do just fine. With any luck you have participated in fashioning a thoughtful transition process and search and have had at least some say about who are the people who will preside over that process. If you participated in those decisions wisely then you should have little reason not to have confidence in them. Several founders we talked with chose not to be on their search committees in part to communicate this confidence; as one founder put it, "I was comfortable with the actions of the search committee. I knew the caliber of people they were considering and that my role was to offer an overall vision for the transition."

Confidence in the new director may very well be an attitude, since you may not have met that person. But clearly the perspective you want to convey is that those in charge of the search are up to the task and the kind of person they select and present will be just fine. Any expressed doubts about this process or its outcomes will have some undermining effect. That kind of action is not up to the standard of leadership required of the founder — paving the way to success and letting go.

C) Factors after succession

7. Briefing and Connecting: The extent to which the founder takes time with the new executive to convey essential information.

Part of this is planning and taking time. Some founders go out the door the day the new executive arrives. But they also have an agreement with the board to continue for a few months as a consultant to their successor as needed. Offering to serve as a consultant can work well because it puts the initiative (and therefore power) with the new executive. Others have planned for an overlapping period of four to six weeks. This method can work well if the founder can let go and do what the new executive wishes and no more. One founder and successor who used an overlap period joked that they were "twins," essentially living a month of the organization's life as dual executives, with responsibilities ranging from directing internal operations to accepting awards for the organization to conducting radio interviews to meeting key constituents.

Clearly there is knowledge that the founder has that would be useful to the new person. The issue is how to convey it in a way that strengthens the executive and diminishes the importance of the founder. Such knowledge will likely be related to issues of budgeting, investments, finance, fundraising, and facilities. That is, it is more likely to do with more factual issues where the founder had primary responsibility. It may be tempting to brief the successor on the staff and board, but it is probably better that the new executive spend personal time to make such discoveries themselves, without your perspective. In fact, one successor we interviewed thought the founder's briefing was not entirely helpful, saying, "I got a very particular viewpoint from the founder which was counterproductive later on."

There are also people to meet. That would include big funders, policy makers, city officials, reporters and editors, and others who have an impact on the life of the organization. Founders who do a gracious hosting and connecting in this regard will be doing an important piece of work for the ongoing well-being of the organization.

8. Post-Departure: Nature of the founding director's ongoing relationship with the staff, board, and new director.

Here we found a variety of scenarios. The key in all of them seemed to be that the new director — not the founder — was the primary determiner of the who, how, and when of this. One new director utilized the founder as a paid personal consultant for six months. Another founding director took a twelve-month leave of absence for board and staff to allow the new executive to get her footing unhampered by the previous leadership. In another the founder departed to an out-of-state position and had little or no contact.

This is more of the leadership of letting go, of getting on with life, of permitting the organization to go forward in new ways and with new leadership — out from under the watchful eye of the founder. The leadership of letting go is likely not an easy challenge after years of shepherding an organization and building personal relationships. However, all the evidence suggests that letting go and allowing the new executive to be the guide in terms of any ongoing involvement is the strategy that will best serve your organization.

Chapter V

For the Successor

This section is for those who follow the founder. While you may have heard that it is the successor to the successor who succeeds, it need not be the case. There is much evidence from our interviews and from the literature that executives who replace founders often do very well, even though it is not a simple matter or as easy as following an incompetent executive or a founder who stayed long beyond the ability to be effective. Achieving such success does require a more than usual level of patience and commitment to listening and learning. It is also true that successors who have a strong sense of themselves, personal confidence, and integrity do better in a situation where some imply, if not ask, that you be and do like your beloved predecessor.

From interviews and experience we identified four factors that influence the success of the transition period for the new executive. These factors have to do with familiarity, criticism, listening, and confluence. A word about each:

1. Familiarity: The extent of knowledge about the agency that the new director has before being hired.

There is much with which the new executive needs to become acquainted in an organization: staff, board, constituents, programs, and administrative procedures and policies, to name a few. Prior knowledge of these greatly affects the learning curve and the new executive's ability to fully engage and lead. Sometimes coming to the organization fresh without prior biases has advantages, but overall familiarity with the people and mission of the organization makes for a shorter and smoother transition period.

2. Criticism: Degree to which the new director talks about and criticizes the founder.

Any new executive will rather quickly discover what the strengths of the previous leader were and exactly what had been done less well. Without question the new executive will inherit things that need at least management attention and perhaps fixing or solving. The fixing and solving categories require time and effort not readily available given all else the executive needs to learn and do. The obvious temptation is to be critical of the founding director for not having tended to these issues. Such criticism, if widely expressed, is likely to have a larger and more negative effect on the organization's assessment of the new executive, rather than their assessment of the recently departed executive. Not a good start. Such criticisms and "what to do about it" conversations are best relegated to the privacy of a trusted confidant.

3. Listening: The time the new director takes to understand before making changes.

Actually this suggests an excellent interview question that should be asked: "Describe what you would do the first one hundred days on the job." If the answer is full of a lot of action steps and change strategies, it probably should not be well-received. Organizations do respond well to movement and progress. They respond far better if the progress is thoughtful and considered. It is fine — even important — for a new director to assemble a new vision for the organization. However, it is unwise to do so on a schedule that causes people to believe you do not fully understand the situation. The operative word here is assemble. That implies hearing from and taking in the insights and hopes of the key constituents. That will not easily be done in less than one hundred days. One successor we spoke with said it took over six months to feel comfortable putting a personal stamp on any part of the organization, while another felt that even several years after the transition there were new things to learn. So keep in mind that while you don't want to take a passive approach to leading, you should keep listening well into your tenure.

4. Confluence: The degree to which the new director already embodies the key aspects of the organization's culture.

This is a subtle one and not easily described. What we do understand is roughly what we mean when we say, "Anne is a natural for that job." It has to do with fit or confluence — the ease with which people can look at the leader and look at the organization and see the match. Leaders who quickly and naturally embody the mission within themselves and who represent the organizational essence in the community have an extra-special strength and validity. When an organization can find such a person who also has the set of abilities the job requires, there is a distinctive confluence that makes for effectiveness as a leader.

Along with these four factors that come from the interviews is some additional wisdom contained in the literature. One author, J.J. Gabarro, outlines five stages of learning and action that we believe may be helpful in the early months of your work:

1. *Taking hold* – a period of orientational and evaluative learning and corrective action

2. *Immersion* – a period of relatively little change but more reflective and penetrating learning

3. *Reshaping* – a period of major change during which the new manager acts on the deeper understanding gained in the preceding stage

4. *Consolidation* – a period in which earlier stages are consolidated

5. *Refinement* – a period of fine-tuning and relatively little major additional learning

These stages will occur during the first two or three years of your position in the organization, and they will enable you to achieve several elements key to success in the new agency. First, they allow you to familiarize yourself with the organization, its strengths, weaknesses, opportunities, and threats. Second, they provide you with opportunities to form relationships with staff, board members, and other key constituents. Finally, they leave room within the transition for you to create the appropriate organizational changes and establish yourself as an effective, capable leader.

Within these stages, there are some particularly important challenges and issues that you will have to face. Such challenges to you as the new executive can come in many forms. Tom Gilmore, in his research on executive succession, suggests what some of these challenges might be.

First, staff members may look carefully for indications that a successor's loyalty lies with their organization and its mission. This is compounded by a successor's tendency to reevaluate his or her decision at moments of doubt; as Gilmore comments, "most new leaders experience moments of doubt about whether they should have taken the new job and feel nostalgia for their old setting."

Second, staff can withhold information necessary for you to make competent decisions out of a fear of losing their strategic advantage. This problem can be overcome by a concerted effort to forge relationships with staff members. As leader you must ensure that employees feel you understand their unique challenges and dilemmas. Further, by accepting a deliberate learner role and with thoughtful and patient listening your credibility will be more easily established. You may wonder whether this strategy will cause you to be co-opted and lose your own sense of direction and integrity. However, that need not be the case at all, and the hazards of not asking, not listening, and remaining aloof are far greater.

Gilmore also outlines three patterns of misunderstanding which can be difficult for you in the early months of your work in the new agency. The first relates to your patterns of delegation. It may be unclear in the early months which issues to address and in what order. The effect of such lack of clarity is that staff members are left in a state of limbo – waiting to do their own end of the work and yet not knowing when or how to begin. This can be further complicated by the early tendency among some staff to consult when they should handle the issue on their own, and, conversely, fail to consult when they should.

A second area of misunderstanding is related to the pattern of attention to internal versus external issues. There will be pressure to differentiate between the internal matters of transition, assimilation, and direction, and external issues of establishing yourself, learning the new professional community, and meeting the needs of diverse constituents. This is an especially key issue since most executives will interact with a wide range of individuals external to the organization on a daily basis.

The third challenge has to do with consultation and resistance to change. This relates directly to your own reasonable desire to effect change and the staff's concerns that these changes will negatively impact them or other aspects of the organization that they believe are going well. In extreme cases resistance to change can take the form of staff taking a defensive attitude towards your leadership — in effect 'circling the wagons' — and making your ability to bring about change nearly impossible through their lack of cooperation.

That would be a most extreme situation. Our own experience from interviews and the literature is that your job as a successor to the founding director does have unique challenges and is one requiring patience and skill. It is also eminently doable and clearly crucial if we are to maintain health and well-being in the community of nonprofit organizations.

Chapter VI
A Final Word

Most of all: lead. The easiest way to operate during a time of change and transition is to just go about doing all that needs to be done. After all, there's plenty for everyone to do, such as the mechanics, logistics, protocol, and procedures involved with learning a new organization. Along these lines we have made suggestions about such processes, checklists, and timelines. But throughout this report we have also hinted at something more. That something more is choosing to be a leader.

For the founding director we have suggested a new kind of leadership. Over the years these founders have exerted a leadership characterized by envisioning, creating, sustaining, and renewing. That is what the early days and those that followed required. Now with the transition underway and departure soon to follow a different kind of leadership is necessary. The executive who was founder must now lead by doing everything possible to prepare the way for the success of those who will take hold of the organization. This leadership of preparing the way is matched only by the leadership of letting go — not an easy matter for one who has so closely guarded and nurtured the mission and life of the organization. But doing anything less — hanging on, even hanging around — communicates a kind of anxiousness, control, and lack of trust that are the antithesis of what it means to lead. In short, the founder needs to lead in new ways.

As for the board's leadership, it's important to recognize that sometimes boards get lulled into passivity by a strong founding director. They end up becoming audience to the executive performer. They do make motions, pass budgets, and approve minutes, but otherwise are content to observe and applaud the high-wire act of the executive. This leadership of low-level engagement will not work for the transition and departure of a founding director. Now is the time to act on the fact that you as the board are charged with holding the mission in trust.

Choosing to lead at this crucial time will mean far more than passing motions and budgets. To start with you can count on the fact that it will require more time. You will want to include the executive but you also will want to make clear that the final responsibility for the transition process is yours. You, after all, are the ones who will remain. You will provide the continuity. You will be entrusted with the ongoing well-being of your organization. And because all that is true, now is the time for you to take charge, to lead, and to show yourselves worthy of being trusted with the life and mission of the organization.

And finally, some additional words of encouragement for the successor: following a founder is no simple matter. It requires a way of leading and a way of being that are distinctive to the tasks of executive leadership. The temptations to be less than what mature leadership requires are many. Some will give in to wanting too quickly to put their own stamp on the organization. Some will fail to patiently understand the essence of the culture, history, and beginnings of the organization. Some will permit themselves glib criticisms of the founder and the way the organization has been shaped or structured. None of these of course inspire confidence or trust in the new leadership. All in fact are failures to lead — to do and be what is best for the organization.

While the challenges of succeeding a founder are substantial there is much evidence that such succession can work very well. It requires more than a usual level of patience and a strong commitment to listening well. It also requires an understanding that there are many ways to run an organization and that the one way to which you are most accustomed may not be the best one for this new situation. In short, leadership is what is required. Leadership is, after all, the art of rising above, looking beyond, seeing and responding to what is most crucial and significant. Successors who succeed exercise that kind of leadership.

Appendix A

Literature Review

While there is no perfect formula for planning a successful transition from founding director to successor, many scholars of management and governance have examined the topic in great detail. What we offer you here is a look at some of the issues these scholars think are important to know about beginning your succession process, potential ways to structure the process itself, and a few hints about how to assess its success or failure. We've identified three issues from the literature we think may relate to your organization's planning and assessment processes leading up to transition: organizational culture, organizational life cycle, and change within non-profits. Then we've outlined two potential approaches taken from the for-profit literature: a transition process and some suggestions from family business literature which both speak to the unique concerns of founding director transition.

Organizational culture

Just as nations have unique cultures, so do organizations and yours is no exception. Organizational culture encompasses the way staff, board, and volunteers view their work, and is first set by a founding director. According to Edgar Schein, a professor emeritus at the Sloan School of Management at MIT and considered by many a founding father of the field of corporate culture, the executive director has primary responsibility for the way an organization's culture develops. In his book *Organizational Culture and Leadership* (1985) Schein comments, "Organizational cultures are created by leaders, and one of the most decisive functions of leadership may well be the creation, the management, and — if and when that may become necessary — the destruction of culture." He adds that the founding director's personal philosophy on leadership and organizational life defines the initial culture from which all others will flow. As your organization plans for leadership transition, you will want to identify the key characteristics of your culture to understand where you have come from and where you might want to go.

Schein defines organizational culture in the following way:

> A pattern of basic assumptions — invented, discovered, or developed by a given group as it learns to cope with its problems of external adaptation and internal integration — that has worked well enough to be considered valid and, therefore, to be taught to new members as the correct way to perceive, think, and feel in relation to these problems.

He points to three ways in which organizational culture is communicated. The first, most obvious way is through what he terms "artifacts" such as the organization's physical space, written and spoken communication, and overt behavior. The second way to understand an organization's culture is through its values, which Schein defines as "convictions about the nature of reality and how to deal with it" usually set by the founder. These values come to be accepted by other members of the organization through a trial-by-fire process; the founder addresses problems using these values as a guide, with the most successful approaches adopted over time by the staff and the board. Schein's third indicator of organizational culture, basic underlying assumptions, serves as "theories-in-use that actually guide behavior, that tell group members how to perceive, think about, and feel about things." He considers these basic underlying assumptions as the essence of the culture, whereas artifacts and values are the surface level manifestations of it.

In *Organizational Rules: A Framework for Understanding Organizational Action* (1991), Albert Mills notes that often organizational culture becomes more influential during moments of challenge — times when the organization faces change, uncertainty, or upheaval. Such moments offer an opportunity to reshape the culture as it is learned or re-learned by organizational members. However, before the successor can begin to shape the culture according to her personal leadership style, she must understand what factors led to its development, the way the organization's current members view it, and how it influences the transition as it occurs.

Organizational life cycle

Your organization's stage of development influences much of the work you do — the size and scope of your programs or services, the level of board, volunteer, and funder involvement, and the way you view both routine and change. All of these, in turn, influence the way you plan for transition. Most likely an organization anticipating founding director transition is in the maturity or prime stage of life, so the model of organizational life presented here serves primarily as an assessment tool to help you read your organization at the time the founder is departing. While it does include death as the final stage of life, organizations routinely cycle through the middle stages of life several times, experiencing decline followed by renewal or even rebirth rather than death, which may be an unlikely event.

Ichak Adizes, founder and director of the Adizes Institute in Los Angeles and Dean of the Adizes Graduate School for Organizational Transformation, presents a layered model of organizational life in his article "Organizational Passages: Diagnosing and Treating Lifecycle Problems of Organizations" (1979). His stages reflect those of human social development:

- Courtship stage
- Infant organization
- Adolescent organization
- Prime organization
- Mature organization
- Aristocratic organization
- Early bureaucracy
- Bureaucracy
- Death

Adizes contrasts the organizational environment before maturity with its environment post-maturity. In the initial four stages, initiative and internal change dominate, employees are hired based upon the skills that will result in the most organizational growth, and "everything is permitted unless specifically forbidden." Once the organization reaches maturity, however, the reverse is true. The organization is dominated by administration, staff are often hired based upon their ability to fit into the existing organizational culture, and "everything is forbidden unless specifically permitted."

Adizes's model places the best moment for major organizational change at the prime stage. At this stage, he points out, the organization has not yet lost its responsiveness to the external environment, a quality which is particularly essential for success in the nonprofit sector. Internally, organizations prior to the maturity phase have greater flexibility to delegate the founder's responsibilities to other organizational members, decreasing dependency on the founder prior to executive transition.

Change in nonprofit organizations

Jacquelyn Wolf, a faculty member at York University and consultant on major change strategies to nonprofit, business, and government organizations, warns against an overly rigid plan for any transition. In her article "Managing Change in Nonprofit Organizations" (1990), she describes organizational change as a process, not an isolated event, which as such should be responsive to emerging needs both internally and externally. Because leadership transition usually takes place over an extended period of time, an organization should develop a transition planning framework rather than a transition plan.

While this approach to change will allow flexibility and responsiveness, it may also create anxieties among staff and board members. They may feel that the plan either lacks sufficient structure to result in successful transition, or that they are not able to contribute to the process without detailed tasks or responsibilities. Many of these anxieties can be avoided by involving some of these individuals in the planning process. This not only allows a variety of organizational members to contribute to the transition in positive ways, it also increases communication throughout the organization about the transition, framing it as an upcoming moment in the organization's life rather than an unknown quantity posing a threat to organizational stability.

A model process from the for-profit sector

Scholars have conducted extensive research on private sector leadership transition, including founding director succession, which offers insight into similar transitions in the nonprofit sector. Rather than provide a template transition process, here we offer several perspectives from this transition literature that we hope will help you design a successful framework that's right for your organization.

In *Making a Leadership Change* (1988), Thomas North Gilmore presents the following eight-stage process for leadership transition:

1. A decision to seek a change in leadership.
2. The design of a search and selection process.
3. An analysis of the strategic challenges to the organization.
4. The translation of the strategic assessment into specific leadership needs and job qualifications.
5. A search for prospective candidates.
6. The screening and initial selection of finalists.
7. The interviewing and final selection of candidates.
8. A transition process.

In most cases, the founding director sets the process in motion by deciding to retire and communicating that decision to board and staff. Gilmore warns that when entering phase two, designing the search and selection process, the organization should guard against 'groupthink' such as turning a blind eye toward organizational negatives and developing an unrealistic view of the executive's job. This can be complicated by a dependency on the founder that is difficult to address; Gilmore notes in one case he studied "the central issue for this organization was overcoming dependency on the founder. But instead of being able to see this issue, the board members were incapacitated by that very dependency." This is yet another reason search and selection committees should include individuals who perform different functions within the organization and who can honestly assess its strengths and weaknesses.

Another potential downfall of 'groupthink' — making field-specific assumptions about where to search for candidates — can limit your applicant pool significantly. The search committee should consider nontraditional sources for potential applicants as well as traditional ones, such as seasoned administrators in the field. Calling key informants — individuals in educational, grant-making, and service organizations who may know of hidden talent — is one way to break into these unexpected areas.

Often search committees inadvertently limit the number of applicants for the founding executive's position by creating an unrealistic description of responsibilities and necessary skills. The founding director's job most often develops around that person's specific abilities and the demands of the environment when the organization was founded. This highly specialized combination of skills may not reappear in another individual, requiring the search committee to rethink the current role of the executive and then, in turn, of other staff members who may be capable of acquiring new responsibilities.

Gilmore considers organizational assessment crucial to the success of a leadership change. Testing the organization's mission, exploring its history, and identifying its culture allows members to learn from the previous leadership, define what parts of the mission still hold true, and change those that need revision, rejuvenation, or elimination.

From family business literature

David Bork's work on family business transitions in *Family Business, Risky Business* (1986) adds important perspective to Gilmore's work as it describes the unique relationship a founder has to his organization. Bork, who is president of a consulting firm that specializes in in-depth counseling and planning for family businesses, points out that in addition to improving the transition process, assessing the organization's culture, life cycle, and mission helps the board, staff, and volunteers understand the need for the organization to be professionalized. This moves attention away from identifying who will take charge to who should take charge. John L. Ward in his book *Keeping the Family Business Healthy* (1987) supports this notion by saying, "the previous generation implemented entrepreneurial strategies by instinct and the need to survive; successors, in contrast, must use planned and conscious administration."

Another key idea presented in family business literature is the need for an articulated organizational history to help future executives, staff, and stake-holders understand how the organization developed over time and where it seems headed. Ward suggests a series of questions designed to uncover important historical information:

- How was the organization founded?
- How were decisions made in the beginning?
- What threats did the organization face? When? How did the organization respond?
- How was the organization organized at the start?
- How has the organization changed?
- Who left the organization and why?

A nonprofit might also ask what unique need in the community led to the organization's founding, how the mission has evolved over time, and who has believed enough in the organization to fund it and why.

In conclusion

In thinking back over the literature discussed in this section, the following are some ways to assess your transition process, including how you will define its success or failure. A good place to start is by identifying some key elements, both internal and external, that will let you know the organization is doing well throughout the transition process. Here are some examples:

Internally

- Do the organization's activities reflect the mission statement, and do the strategic goals and directions work to achieve that mission?

- Do the staff, board, funders, and volunteers feel confident about the organization — its activities, its directives, and its positioning — under the new leader?

- Does the organization's product — whether education, programming, art, or services — remain high quality?

Externally

- Has the organization maintained (or even increased) its position and reputation within the community?

- Have funders continued their relationship with the organization? Do they feel confidence in the organization and express satisfaction with the benefits they receive from that relationship?

- Does the audience or served population feel a similar comfort level with the organization's product, in that they are pleased with any changes or have not perceived any?

- Has the organization weathered environmental changes effectively?

These are questions that could be usefully addressed during the planning process, the last days of the founder, the first days of the new executive, or sometime during the continuing days of the new executive.

Additional Recommended Reading

Adizes, I. (1979). Organizational passages: Diagnosing and treating lifecycle problems of organizations. *Organizational Dynamics*, 8 (1), 3-25.

Bennis, W. & Nanus, B. (1985). *Leadership: strategies for taking charge.* New York: Harper Collins.

Berenbeim, R.E. (1984). *From owner to professional management: Problems in transition.* New York: The Conference Board.

Bork, D. (1986). *Family business, risky business: How to make it work.* New York: American Management Association.

Bork, D., Jaffe, D.T., Lane, S.H., Dashew, L., & Heisler, Q.G. *Working with family businesses: A guide for professionals.* San Francisco: Jossey-Bass Inc.

Enz, C.A. (1986). *Power and shared values in the corporate culture.* Ann Arbor, Michigan: UMI Research Press.

Gabarro, J.J. (1987). *The dynamics of taking charge.* Boston: Harvard Business School Press.

Gilmore, T.N. (1988). *Making a leadership change: How organizations and leaders can handle leadership transitions successfully.* San Francisco: Jossey-Bass Inc.

Gray, B., & Ariss, S.S. (1985). Politics and strategic change across organizational life cycles. *Academy of Management Review*, 10 (4), 707-723.

Kets de Vries, M.F.R. (1995). *Organizational paradoxes: Clinical approaches to management* (2nd ed.). New York: Routledge.

Kets de Vries, M.F.R. (1993). The dynamics of family controlled firms: The good and the bad news. *Organizational Dynamics*, 21 (3), 59-71.

Mills, A.J. & Murgatroyd, S.J. (1991). *Organizational rules: A framework for understanding organizational action.* Philadelphia: Open University Press.

Schein, E.H. (1985). *Organizational culture and leadership.* San Francisco: Jossey-Bass Inc.

Ward, J.L. (1987). *Keeping the family business healthy.* San Francisco: Jossey-Bass Inc.

Wolf, J. (1990). Managing change in nonprofit organizations. In D.L. Gies, J.S. Ott, & J.M. Shafritz (Eds.), *The nonprofit organization: Essential readings* (pp. 241-257). Belmont, CA: Wadsworth Publishing Co.

Appendix B
Methodology

Three types of information form the basis of the findings in this report: a review of scholarly literature on nonprofit management and executive transition, interviews with members of organizations who have experienced founding director transition, and written planning and transition documents from these same organizations. All the drafts of the findings were reviewed by a project committee consisting of two founding executives, two experienced nonprofit board members, and a graduate student who is also a nonprofit administration professional. Their ideas, insights, and constructive criticisms ground the results you see here.

The literature search covers research done over the past 20 years primarily by academicians in the field of management, some business and some nonprofit. Because nonprofit management is an emerging field, we were able to find information on basic issues such as strategic planning, assessment, and organizational characteristics, but to find insights on specific management issues such as transition we needed to look elsewhere. We found this information in for-profit literature on executive transition, which offers helpful guidelines to designing a process in a nonprofit organization. We found insight into the issue of succession with a founding director in family business literature. Family businesses tend to be small, personal operations that are initially run in much the same way as a new nonprofit. Transitioning to professional management outside the family presents many challenges similar to those of founding director transition.

The interviews included five organizations, all literary centers in the nation's Midwest region: The Guild Complex, Just Buffalo, The Loft, The Thurber House, and Woodland Pattern. Three of these organizations had already completed founding director transitions when the interviews took place. Of the remaining two, one will have completed transition by this report's publication, and the other has begun its transition planning process. We interviewed four founding directors, five current executives, six board members, and seven staff members. Each interview was approximately one hour in length and while we did use an informal interview schedule, we allowed for a great deal of flexibility in our conversations in order to get the best insights from each person.

The planning and transition documents for some organizations were comprehensive, for some were available in part, and for others were non-existent. We used the available documents as a guide to understanding each organization's unique approach to the transition process and included an excerpt of one as a potential model.

As mentioned in the introduction, this research is qualitative case study research. That means that while our data collection process combines both scholarly and field research, we do not claim that we can generalize the results to every case. We studied similar organizations so they could be easily compared and we spoke with a large group of people to ensure our results were representative. We think that the information we have collected is a good and solid start to transition planning and combines some of the best that academicians and practitioners have to offer on the subject.